# HISTORY AND GEOGRAPHY
# THE SEARCH FOR PEACE

## CONTENTS

Author:        Alpha Omega Staff
Editor:        Alan Christopherson M. S.
Illustrations: Alpha Omega Staff

Alpha Omega Publications®

804 N. 2nd Ave. E., Rock Rapids, IA 51246-1759
© MM by Alpha Omega Publications, Inc.   All rights reserved.
LIFEPAC is a registered trademark of Alpha Omega Publications, Inc.

# HISTORY 1107
# THE SEARCH FOR PEACE

Suspicion and distrust among nations on the European mainland reached the breaking point in 1914 when Serbian-Austrian relations collapsed. This event set off a chain reaction of active and reactive involvement as Europe and the world embarked on the first global conflict. The United States strove to remain neutral, but was drawn into the conflict of World War I, supplying the men and equipment that brought the war to a close and the Allies to victory.

After World War I the United States departed from Wilson's progressivism and entered into Harding's restoration of "normalcy." Although the United States had enhanced its prosperity and its position of respect in the world community, the nation was ill-prepared for the shock of 1929. When the stock market crashed, thousands of people were left destitute; the subsequent years of the Great Depression also took their toll. The administration of Franklin Roosevelt brought practical promises and positive actions, giving hope to the confused and stricken people of the United States.

In this unit you will study the triumph, confusion, and desperation in the history of our nation between 1914 and 1940. The major focal points of your study will include the role of the United States in World War I, the aftermath of that conflict, the return to normal times, the prosperous living of the twenties, the dark days of the Great Depression, and America's struggle under the Roosevelt administration to overcome the economic stagnation.

United States history can be seen as a drama of our nation's will to triumph over seemingly insurmountable obstacles in a struggle for independence, unity, stability, and respect. The segment of that history from 1914 to 1940 included the vital learning experiences of global warfare, postwar difficulties, and economic depths, each contributing to the present stature of the United States.

## OBJECTIVES

**Read these objectives.** The objectives tell you what you will be able to do when you have successfully completed this LIFEPAC®.

When you have finished this LIFEPAC, you should be able to:

1. Describe the opposing forces and their engagements on the European front in World War I.

2. Describe the Unites States' war effort at home and abroad.

3. Outline the plans for world peace at the close of World War I.

4. Describe the changing postwar attitudes as the United States returned to normalcy.

5. Explain the effects of urbanization and prohibition on United States' society.

6. Outline the philosophy and policies of Coolidge.

7. Describe the prosperity and disaster of the Hoover years.

8. Describe the effects of the Great Depression on the United States' wealthy and poor.

9. Explain the effects of Franklin D. Roosevelt's leadership on recovery in the United States during the depression years.

**Survey the LIFEPAC.** Ask yourself some questions about this study. Write your questions here.

_____

_____

_____

_____

_____

_____

_____

_____

_____

_____

_____

_____

_____

# I. THE GREAT WAR AND ITS AFTERMATH

Although hostilities eventually extended around the world, most of the decisive action in the Great War—World War I—took place on the European continent. Europe is also the place where the subsequent peace talks were negotiated. Therefore, the focus of your study in this section will be on the European continent, noting the rising tension and hostilities among those nations, the unavoidable involvement of the United States, and the proposals and terms for a hopeful world peace.

## SECTION OBJECTIVES

**Review these objectives.** When you have completed this section, you should be able to:

1. Describe the opposing forces and their engagements on the European front in World War I:

   1.1 List the Allied and Central Powers, telling how each became involved in the war.

   1.2 Outline the war strategies on the European front.

2. Describe the United States' war effort at home and abroad:

   2.1 Describe the measures taken on the home front in support of the war effort.

   2.2 Tell the advantages the United States supplied to the Allied cause.

3. Outline the plans for world peace at the close of World War I:

   3.1 List the terms and effects of Wilson's Fourteen Points.

   3.2 List the terms and effects of the Treaty of Versailles.

## VOCABULARY

**Study these words** to enhance your learning success in this section.

| | |
|---|---|
| **armistice** | A temporary end of hostilities by mutual agreement; a truce |
| **reparations** | Money paid by the defeated countries for acts of war |
| **stalemate** | A deadlock or tie |
| **vengeance** | An act of revenge for a wrong or injury |

**Note**: All vocabulary words in this LIFEPAC appear in **boldface** print the first time they are used. If you are unsure of the meaning when you are reading, study the definitions given.

## THE FIRST GLOBAL CONFLICT

World War I was called the Great War before World War II reduced its claim to that title. It was the first world-wide war using modern weapons. Airplanes were used for the first time, mainly for reconnaissance. Tanks were introduced, although they were not highly effective. Poison gas was also used, killing and blinding many. Moreover, this was a war that destroyed civilian lives. War was no longer a disagreement between armies, it was a contest for survival among nations, in this case, mainly the nations of Europe.

**The antagonists of Europe.** The first global conflict began as a result of the assassination of the heir to the Austrian throne, Archduke Francis Ferdinand, and his wife by a member of a Serbian secret society on June 18, 1914. Furious at the brazen actions of this small Balkan nation, Austria was determined to punish Serbia (a Russian ally) severely for the assassination. Being assured of German backing if Russia should support Serbia, the Austrians issued an ultimatum to Serbia—meet Austrian demands concerning the anti-Austrian movement in Serbia or face war. When the Serbs agreed to only partially meet the Austrian demands, Austria declared war on Serbia.

Austria's declaration of war initiated a chain reaction among European nations because of the previously negotiated alliances throughout the continent. Russia, pledging to aid the Serbian government, refused to stop her mobilization in defense of the Serbs when Germany ordered her to halt. Thus, Germany declared war on Russia and its ally, France. Determined to defeat France before Russia was prepared to fight, Germany ignored the neutrality of Belgium and boldly marched across the Belgian border enroute to France.

The conquest of Belgium caused an international uproar toward Germany and hastened Great Britain's decision to join forces with France and Russia. Realizing that the only possible gains in war would come from Austrian-controlled territories, Italy joined the war in 1915 as an ally of Russia, France, and England. Italy's new alignment was a shocking blow to her former partners in the Triple Alliance.

Nation by nation, battle lines were drawn. Turkey joined the Central Powers (Germany, Austria-Hungary), giving Germany and Austria control of Constantinople and blockading the Russian fleet stationed in the Black Sea. In 1914 Japan entered the war on the side of Great Britain in accordance with their previous treaty, the Anglo-Japanese Alliance of 1902. Countries throughout the world were soon armed for the global confrontation, World War I. Few European nations remained uninvolved; only Switzerland, Spain, Holland, and the Scandinavian countries declared their neutrality.

In their move to take France, the Germans did not consider the bravery and genius of the French. In a desperate move, French soldiers were driven in taxi cabs from Paris to the front line to stop the German advance. This heroic action halted the surprised German troops and was soon followed by a stiff French counterattack, saving Paris and stalling German hopes for a quick victory.

Although French resistance was much stronger than Germany had expected, Germany had little difficulty overcoming Russian resistance. Poor equipment, disorganized supply lines, and weak leadership contributed to the defeat and containment of the Russian forces by the well-equipped, disciplined Germans. When the Allies (Great Britain, France, Russia, Serbia, Belgium, Japan, Montenegro) were defeated in their efforts to aid the battered Russians, Germany grew confident in its strong, strategic military position in Central Europe.

**German U-Boat**

By 1916 the war had reached a **stalemate**. Much of the land war was fought in trenches where little ground was gained and many lives were lost. At sea, German submarines (U-boats) sank shipments of supplies destined for England and France. The French and British navies blockaded the North Sea to prevent supplies from reaching Germany. Neither side had a clear advantage that could break the stalemate, and both sides were suffering heavy losses and growing weary of war. Nevertheless, the impasse could not last forever; and both sides were desperate in their attempts to enlist additional support. Propaganda flooded the United States, taking advantage of the intense interest with which sympathizers were watching both sides.

**German Warfare**

5

**Woodrow Wilson**

**The role of the United States.** The United States had declared neutrality from the beginning of the war. President Woodrow Wilson had strong support from the people when he said, "The war is one with which we have nothing to do, whose causes cannot touch us." Wilson also said that the United States would remain free to "do what is honest ...and truly serviceable for the peace of the world."

Although such thinking was noble, idealistic, and certainly desirable, it proved to be only illusionary. In spite of public opinion, the United States had to make a decision and choose sides. Although German-Americans supported the Central Powers, most citizens in the United States were pro-British and supported the Triple Entente (France, Great Britain, Russia) and the Allied powers. Propaganda was widely used by both sides in the conflict, but French and British data was far more convincing to the United States public. However, the United States was not drawn into global war through propaganda tactics; it entered the war because Germany was sinking American supply ships heading for England and France.

Looking at the situation from Germany's viewpoint, the indiscriminate sinking of ships was an expedient tactic. Germany would either lose the war on the seas or risk driving the United States into the massive conflict. The United States complained about the German activities and continued to trade with Great Britain. This tense situation was aggravated on May 7, 1915, when a British passenger ship, the *Lusitania*, was sunk by a German U-boat, killing 128 American citizens. When President Wilson sternly rebuked the Germans for the tragedy, Berlin answered with an apology, assuring that such an incident would not happen again. Although a temporary halt was enacted, the Germans later resumed sinking American ships in British waters, killing many Americans. Convinced that the United States could prevent a German victory, President Wilson went to Congress with a war message. Congress responded on April 6, 1917, by declaring war on Germany.

The entrance of the United States into the war gave the Triple Entente and their allies a tremendous boost in morale. Although training troops for the battlefield takes time, by the end of the war in November of 1918, more than two million United States soldiers were in France. The United States had been preparing some for the possibility of war since the early days of European tension.

Industry was especially affected, being influenced by the war's surging production demands and stimulated by President Wilson's request for a United States naval build-up. To meet any possible future challenge, the Committee on Industrial Preparedness had been created to enhance the military resources of the United States. A War Industries Board was also developed to oversee and control the production of manufactured goods within the United States. Given strong advisory power, the Board increased national production to include additional military needs.

WWI

WAR PHOTOGRAPHY

**I WANT YOU FOR U.S.ARMY**

NEAREST RECRUITING STATION

Although the United States navy had been increased and was well prepared for action, the army was small, ill-equipped, and poorly trained. The problem of staffing the armed services was alleviated by the Selective Service Act. This act was passed to draft eligible men between the ages of twenty-one and thirty into the armed forces. The act eventually was expanded to include men between the ages of eighteen and forty-five. Many men volunteered for military duty. Almost five million men served in the armed forces during World War I, and over one million took part in front-line duty in Europe.

Many generals of the Entente wanted to integrate the United States troops into European armies; however, General John J. Pershing, leader of the United States troops, was determined to keep his troops as an independent force. United States servicemen chose the battle song "Over There" as their theme and determined that they would not return home until, "it's over, over there."

The Germans desperately tried to end the war before the Allies were reinforced by fresh American troops by conducting major offensives on their western front in the spring and summer of 1918. Germany was able to send more troops to France because of the Communist Revolution in Russia, which caused the Russians to withdraw from the war in 1917. The German offensive was nearly fatal for the Allies. However, United States troops and supplies poured onto the battlefield in northeastern France just in time. Reinforced by the United States, the Allies' counterattack was successful. Strategic Allied victories included the battle at Cantigny, the Argonne Forest, and Chateau-Thierry. These victories resulted largely from the freshly trained *doughboys* (soldiers) from the United States.

The United States also contributed to the defeat of the Central Powers by generously supplying the Allies with food, ammunition, troops, and other war needs. Citizens in the United States manifested a spirit of sacrifice by often giving up food or gas that could be used to help the war effort in Europe.

American soldiers and supplies poured into Europe's battleground and halted the fierce German offensives of 1918. The Allied counterattacks dealt a severe blow to the German resistance and morale. As their German partners were being pushed steadily back, Bulgaria and Turkey saw no hope for victory and asked for peace. Austria-Hungary split into two separate countries when a peaceful revolution ended that empire. With its allies retreating from the war, Germany foresaw the inevitable invasion of its homeland. Germany signed an **armistice** on November 11, 1918, following several days of negotiations.

**WESTERN FRONT 1914-1918**

| Armistice Line 1918 | Allied offensive Fall 1918 |
| German offensive summer 1918 | Farthest German advance 1914 |
| Beginning of Frontline 1915 | |

**EASTERN FRONT 1914-1918**

Farthest Austria-German advance 1918

Russian front 1917

Gallipoli campaign 1915

Farthest Russian advance 1914

**Choose the best answer(s).**

1.1    Which four things were true of World War I?

_____ a.  By 1916, it was a stalemate in the west
_____ b.  Russia did not fight well
_____ c.  Much of the fighting was done from trenches
_____ d.  Italy fought with the Central Powers
_____ e.  Britain blockaded Germany

1.2    The three nations siding with Russia included:

_____ a.  France
_____ b.  Turkey
_____ c.  Bulgaria
_____ d.  Italy
_____ e.  Japan

1.3    Four neutral nations included:

_____ a.  Switzerland
_____ b.  Spain
_____ c.  Serbia
_____ d.  Scandinavia
_____ e.  Holland
_____ f.  Serbia

1.4    Three measures passed to meet America's wartime needs included:

_____ a.  the Committee on Industrial Preparedness
_____ b.  the Selective Service Act
_____ c.  the War Industries Board
_____ d.  the Industrial Production Council

1.5    Indicate three areas United States reinforcements contributed greatly to Allied victories in France:

_____ a.  Catigny
_____ b.  Berlin
_____ c.  Argonne Forest
_____ d.  Chateau-Thierry

1.6    Four things the United States supplied the Allies with were:

_____ a.  manpower
_____ b.  food
_____ c.  a boost in morale
_____ d.  submarines
_____ e.  military equipment

1.7    Indicate five events leading to the German signing of an armistice:

_____ a.  the collapse of Bulgaria
_____ b.  Turkey's surrender
_____ c.  French peace
_____ d.  the split of Austria-Hungary
_____ e.  Allies forcing a German retreat
_____ f.  a threat to the German homeland

**Fill in the blanks.**

1.8    A temporary end of hostilities by mutual agreement or a truce is called an _____ .

1.9    A deadlock or tie is called a _____ .

**True/False.**

1.10    _____ World War I erupted when an Austrian assassinated Archduke Francis Ferdinand.

1.11    _____ Austria insisted on controlling the anti-Austrian movement in Serbia.

1.12    _____ When Austria declared war on Serbia, Russia came to Serbia's defense.

1.13    _____ Germany received international approval by crossing neutral Belgium to invade France.

1.14    _____ The United States joined the war when Germany crossed neutral Belgium

1.15    _____ Supplies were cut off from Britain by a naval blockade of warships.

1.16    _____ The war was the first global conflict.

1.17    _____ Germany and Austria-Hungary were known as the Allied Powers.

1.18    _____ Britain joined the Allies because of the German defiance of Belgian neutrality.

1.19    _____ Japan sided with Britain because of an Alliance agreed upon in 1904.

**Answer the following question.**

1.20    What caused the United States to enter into World War I?

    _____

    _____

    _____

    _____

    _____

**Adult Check** _____

           **Initial**        **Date**

# A PLAN FOR PEACE

The task of formulating a peace agreement was not an easy one. The majority of the world's people longed for a treaty that would bring lasting peace. The four years of harsh, bitter fighting had affected most major areas of the globe. Although very idealistic, Woodrow Wilson's statements "a war to end all wars" and "a world safe for democracy" expressed the desires of people throughout the world. The Fourteen Points, a peace proposal introduced by Wilson, and the Treaty of Versailles brought a peace. However, it would only settle the issue of war for twenty years.

**Wilson's Fourteen Points.** Before the war ended, President Wilson made a speech to Congress stating his Fourteen Points for a world peace settlement. His views clearly reflected American values:

1. "open covenants openly arrived at," with no secret international agreements in the future;

2. freedom of the seas outside territorial waters in peace and war, except in the case of international action to enforce international treaties;

3. removal of all possible economic barriers and establishment of equal trade conditions among nations;

4. reduction of national armaments to the lowest point consistent with domestic safety;

5. impartial adjustments of colonial claims;

6. evacuation of all German troops from Russia, an opportunity for Russia independently to determine its own political development and national policy and acceptance of Russia as a free nation;

7. evacuation and restoration of Belgium;

8. restoration of France and return of Alsace-Lorraine to France;

9. readjustment of the Italian frontier;

10. limited self-government for the people of Austria-Hungary;

11. reconstruction of Balkan states with access to the sea and independence guaranteed for the Balkan countries;

12. self-determination for Turkey and guarantees that the Dardanelles be permanently opened as a free passage to ships of all nations;

13. independence for Poland and an outlet to the sea; and

14. formation of a general association of nations.

Wilson's Fourteen Points clearly expressed to people around the world that the war would not be fought in vain. Allied soldiers were encouraged by these statements, understanding them as definite goals to defend. Copies of Wilson's proposals were dropped behind German lines and were broadcast by radio into Germany in an effort to make Germany's surrender easier and halt any additional bloodshed.

Popular support seemed to favor the adoption of the Fourteen Points; however, secret treaties were being made with little acknowledgment of Wilson's proposals. When the Germans signed the armistice on November 11, 1918, halting fighting until a peace treaty was signed, they hoped to receive this peace according to Wilson's Fourteen Points. However, as losers, the Germans had no bargaining position and had no guarantee of receiving the items Wilson was seeking.

The peace conference was held on January 18, 1919. Diplomats from the Allied countries met in Paris to draw up a peace treaty with the Germans. Several difficult problems confronted the diplomats; satisfying all the parties involved was almost an impossible task. Many boundary disputes had to be settled, and the many nationalistic groups pressed for a settlement favorable to their own interests. Another sensitive area of negotiations was that of **reparations**. Most of the war fought in Western Europe had taken place in France and Belgium; therefore, someone would have to pay for rebuilding the cities and industries of both these nations. Wilson's points not only dealt with these vital issues, but also offered ideas for securing world peace through the participation of nations in a world-wide organization. Six of his points were of a general nature while eight pertained to specific countries and areas, such as Russia, Belgium, Alsace-Lorraine, and Italy.

President Wilson's efforts were severely tested. His desire for a peace with justice was not shared by the Allied leaders. Wilson fervently believed that fair treatment of all nations involved would prevent new hostilities and hatred from recurring and would act as a deterrent to future conflicts. However, many Allied leaders disagreed with him. In their minds the Central Powers needed to be punished and disciplined for what they had done. Stiff, harsh treatment would be an efficient deterrent from future wars for the Germans and their allies. Because they did not trust the Germans, the French desired to divide, separate, and completely disarm Germany. Thus, the Germans would be so thoroughly defeated they could never fight another war.

As the time for the peace conference in Paris neared, two opposing points of view arose regarding the issue of German treatment: one favoring Wilson's idea of a *just peace* and one favoring a *peace with* **vengeance**. The outcome of the conference was so critical to President Wilson that he personally traveled to France in an effort to ensure that as many of his ideas as possible were adopted.

**Treaty of Versailles.** More than thirty Allied countries were represented at the peace meetings held in Paris in January of 1919. Russia was in the midst of a civil war at that time and was the only major Allied nation not represented at the meetings. Of course, none of the defeated countries were present at the conference.

The decisions on the treaty were made separately by the representatives of the five great powers present: Britain, France, Italy, the United States, and Japan. The remaining national representatives took part in the public writing of the peace treaty.

The true feelings of the major nations concerning the peace settlement quickly rose to the surface. Although Prime Minister David Lloyd George of Great Britain, Premier Vittorio Orlando of Italy, and Premier Georges Clemenceau of France outwardly had expressed agreement to the Fourteen Points, inwardly they backed treaties of vengeance.

**The Big Four**

Wilson believed his idea of a League of Nations was vital to lasting peace and spent much of his time in Paris working on the formation of such an international organization. His efforts were accepted unanimously by the Allied representatives. Thus, the League of Nations was established for the purpose of regulating international relations, limiting armaments, and settling disagreements between nations in a peaceful way.

After his initial success, President Wilson did not fare well in the conference. As the peace meetings progressed, the advocates of a harsh peace became more entrenched in their position. France, Italy, Japan, and Great Britain demanded to be awarded territories and colonies of the Central Powers. Though physically ill and disappointed by the outcome of the meeting, Wilson signed the treaty. His only consolation was that his League of Nations had been adopted.

With bitter reservations, the German government approved the treaty in May of 1919. The representatives of the new German republic signed the treaty on June 18, 1919, at the Palace of Versailles outside Paris. However, they were greatly disturbed because the Fourteen Points were not followed as anticipated, and the obligations for making reparations were vague (later listed at $33 billion).

Under the terms of the treaty, the Germans were forced to give up much territory. Alsace-Lorraine was given to France; Poland, Belgium, and Denmark each received German territory; and the German colonies were divided among the victorious nations. Not only was Germany occupied by foreign troops, but her own army and navy were also drastically reduced. Other Central Powers had their lands divided by the Treaty of Versailles; Austria, Hungary, Bulgaria, and Turkey were thus reduced by the treaty's terms. At the conclusion of World War I, an entire continent had been reshaped. Bitter feelings and unsettled disputes were created that would continue for many years and would eventually resurface.

When the United States voted against joining the League of Nations, it took away much of the confidence other nations had placed in the League. Wilson had predicted a second world war if the League were rejected. Twenty years later, his predictions came true. (although the failure of the League of Nations was not the primary cause of the next war.) Man throughout the ages has sought peace; but as long as this present world stands, man will not find a lasting peace in his own institutions. Jesus gives man an inner peace that the world and its peace treaties cannot provide.

---

**True/False.**

1.21 _____ Wilson's Fourteen Points concerned a world peace settlement following World War II.

1.22 _____ The Fourteen Points were dropped behind enemy lines to encourage surrender.

1.23 _____ The Fourteen Points encouraged the Allied soldiers by giving them goals for which to fight.

1.24 _____ France and Britain needed to receive reparations for the heavy destruction of their land during the war.

1.25 _____ Wilson's peace plans received more support than he had first hoped.

**Select the letters of the three elements that describe the following views concerning treatment of the Central Powers, especially Germany, after the war.**

1.26    a *just peace*

    \_\_\_\_\_  a.  fair treatment of all nations involved
    \_\_\_\_\_  b.  dividing of land
    \_\_\_\_\_  c.  disarming the losing countries
    \_\_\_\_\_  d.  prevent future hostilities
    \_\_\_\_\_  e.  limit bitter feelings
    \_\_\_\_\_  f.  stiff and harsh treatment of Central Powers


1.27    a *peace with vengeance*

    \_\_\_\_\_  a.  fair treatment of all nations involved
    \_\_\_\_\_  b.  dividing of land
    \_\_\_\_\_  c.  disarming the losing countries
    \_\_\_\_\_  d.  prevent future hostilities
    \_\_\_\_\_  e.  limit bitter feelings
    \_\_\_\_\_  f.  stiff and harsh treatment of Central Powers


**Match these items with their best descriptions.**

1.28    \_\_\_\_\_  Treaty of Versailles          a.  organization to secure world peace

1.29    \_\_\_\_\_  Alsace-Lorraine              b.  Wilson's peace plan

1.30    \_\_\_\_\_  Fourteen Points              c.  peace ending World War I

1.31    \_\_\_\_\_  League of Nations            d.  Italian premier

1.32    \_\_\_\_\_  Lloyd George                 e.  French premier

1.33    \_\_\_\_\_  Clemenceau                   f.  disputed French-German territory

1.34    \_\_\_\_\_  Orlando                      g.  British prime minister


**Fill in the blanks.**

1.35    An act of revenge for a wrong or injury is called _____ .

1.36    Money paid by the defeated countries for acts of war is the definition for

    _____ .

**Choose the best answer.**

1.37    Allied countries represented at the Paris peace talks included all of the following *except*:
_____    a.    Britain
_____    b.    Russia
_____    c.    France
_____    d.    United States
_____    e.    Italy
_____    f.    Japan

1.38    Allied heads of government at the peace talks included all of the following *except*:
_____    a.    Lloyd George
_____    b.    Wilson
_____    c.    Clemenceau
_____    d.    Orlando
_____    e.    Wilhelm II

1.39    The League of Nations was established to:
_____    a.    regulate international relations
_____    b.    cease imperialism
_____    c.    increase armaments
_____    d.    settle monetary problems

1.40    Measures taken against Germany by the Treaty of Versailles did *not* include:
_____    a.    French control of Alsace-Lorraine
_____    b.    occupation of Germany
_____    c.    division of German colonies
_____    d.    reduction of German armed forces
_____    e.    Wilson's Fourteen Points

1.41    When the United States voted against joining the League of Nations:
_____    a.    the other nations lost some confidence in the League
_____    b.    the League increased its effectiveness
_____    c.    the president was greatly encouraged
_____    d.    isolation was ended

Review the material in this section in preparation for the Self Test. The Self Test will check your mastery of this particular section. The items missed on this Self Test will indicate specific areas where restudy is needed for mastery.

# SELF TEST 1

**Match these items with the most appropriate descriptions** (each answer, 2 points).

| | | |
|---|---|---|
| 1.01 | _____ Ferdinand | a. originator of League of Nations |
| 1.02 | _____ Wilson | b. British ship sunk by German U-boat |
| 1.03 | _____ *Lusitania* | c. British Prime Minister, World War I |
| 1.04 | _____ Pershing | d. French premier during peace talks |
| 1.05 | _____ Alsace-Lorraine | e. site for signing of peace treaty |
| 1.06 | _____ Versailles | f. French-German disputed territory |
| 1.07 | _____ Central Powers | g. Austrian Archduke who was assassinated |
| 1.08 | _____ Allied Powers | h. Britain, France, Russia |
| 1.09 | _____ Lloyd George | i. Germany and Austria-Hungary |
| 1.010 | _____ Clemenceau | j. commander of American forces in World War I |

**Match the following events with their significance in history** (each answer, 2 points).

| | | |
|---|---|---|
| 1.011 | _____ assassination of Ferdinand | a. oversee and control war-time manufacturing |
| 1.012 | _____ German march across Belgium | b. organization proposed by Wilson for peaceful settlement of world problems |
| 1.013 | _____ sinking of *Lusitania* | c. incident that pushed the U.S. closer to war with Germany |
| 1.014 | _____ surrender of Turkey and Bulgaria | d. led to the British entrance in the war on France's side |
| 1.015 | _____ Treaty of Versailles | e. a plan of fair treatment of all nations to prevent further hostilities |
| 1.016 | _____ War Industries Board | f. influenced German surrender |
| 1.017 | _____ Fourteen Points | g. harsh restriction of Germany through terms of peace treaty |
| 1.018 | _____ League of Nations | h. Wilson's plan for lasting peace after World War I |
| 1.019 | _____ just peace | i. brought peace at the end of World War I |
| 1.020 | _____ peace of vengeance | j. led to the Austrian declaration of war on Serbia and sparked World War I |

**True/False** (each answer, 2 points).

1.021     _____ Austria demanded the right to handle the anti-Austrian movement in Serbia.

1.022     _____ When Germany defied the French neutrality, Britain entered the war.

1.023     _____ World War I ground fighting took place in trenches.

1.024     _____ Naval blockades and/or submarine warfare interfered with supplies going to both sides in the war.

1.025     _____ Although the United States army was well prepared for war, her navy was ill-equipped.

1.026     _____ Pershing agreed with Allied generals to integrate American troops into the European armies.

1.027     _____ The American reinforcements reached northeastern France in time to prevent the German offensive from being successful.

1.028     _____ The Germans hoped for a peace according to the Fourteen Points.

1.029     _____ During the Paris peace talks, more nations favored a just peace than a peace of vengeance.

1.030     _____ The League of Nations was rejected by the United States.

**Choose the best answer** (each answer, 2 points).

1.031     A nation that remained neutral in World War I was: \_\_\_\_\_ .
    a. the United States
    b. Belgium
    c. Japan
    d. Switzerland
    e. Italy

1.032     World War I included all of the following *except*: \_\_\_\_\_ .
    a. German submarine warfare
    b. Japan fighting as a British ally
    c. Turkey fighting as a Germany ally
    d. Russia withdrawing after the Communist Revolution
    e. A just and fair peace treaty

1.033     The United States did not supply the Allied cause with: \_\_\_\_\_ .
    a. food, munitions and supplies
    b. a plan for peace
    c. new territory in Austria-Hungary
    d. reinforcement of troops

1.034     Events leading to the German surrender included all of the following *except*: \_\_\_\_\_ .
    a. collapse of Turkey and Bulgaria
    b. United States joining the Allies
    c. split of Austria-Hungary
    d. Allies forcing the German retreat
    e. threat to the German homeland
    f. surrender of Russia

1.035      The Treaty of Versailles forced Germany to: _____ .
a. keep Alsace-Lorraine
b. occupy Poland
c. accept Wilson's Fourteen Points
d. reduce its army and navy
e. keep the old German colonies

**Fill in the blank** (each answer, 3 points).

1.036      The United States eventually entered World War I because German U-boats sank ships with
_____ aboard.

58 / 73

Score
Adult Check

_____
_____
Initial      Date

# II. THE GOLDEN TWENTIES

After the exhaustive war effort, the United States needed to return to a normal state of affairs. Americans were ready to leave behind the sacrifices and demands of a wartime existence, to center their efforts and interests around their own betterment and prosperity. President Harding's "Back to Normalcy" motto was associated with a national emphasis on internal affairs. As a consequence of this perspective, the nation favored a movement toward disarmament and withdrawal from international organizations. New immigration quotas were established to restrict the number of incoming foreigners. The quality of life also became a concern to the citizens of the United States. People began moving to the cities to enhance their standard of living, and **Prohibition** was instituted as a means of improving the national life.

## SECTION OBJECTIVES

**Review these objectives.** When you have completed this section, you should be able to:

4.  Describe the changing postwar attitudes as the United States returned to normalcy:

    4.1   Define Wilson's progressivism.

    4.2   List the steps Harding took concerning peace, disarmament, and immigration as he sought to return to a normal state of affairs.

5.  Explain the effects of urbanization and prohibition on United States society:

    5.1   Describe the causes, effects, and movements of urbanization.

    5.2   Give the positive and negative effects of Prohibition.

## VOCABULARY

**Study these words** to enhance your learning success in this section.

| | |
|---|---|
| **bootlegging** | Making or selling liquor illegally |
| **disarmament** | The elimination or limitation of armed forces, military equipment, or weapons of war |
| **hedonistic** | The pursuit of pleasure as the chief activity of life |
| **isolationism** | The thinking that opposes a nation's involvement in political or military affairs outside its hemisphere |
| **progressivism** | The promotion of new and more liberal ideas and changes |
| **Prohibition** | The movement banning the buying and selling of liquor |
| **urbanization** | The growth of city living |

# CHANGING POSTWAR ATTITUDES

Although President Wilson had done an effective job in leading the United States through World War I, its citizens sought a change from the progressive reforms his administration had supported. They looked for a more conservative man, Warren G. Harding, to lead them back to a peacetime lifestyle. As President Wilson prepared to leave the White House, he was aware of the fact that the **progressivism** he supported was rapidly fading in popularity among the people.

By the end of World War I, the people of the United States were weary of the conflict and ready for a time of peace. Nevertheless, many people were concerned about the recent takeover by the Communists in Russia during the Revolution of 1917. Communism appeared as a danger to the security of countries around the world. However, the citizens of the United States wanted to believe the prevailing notion that World War I was truly "the war to end all wars."

**Rejection of progressivism.** Progressivism had been a movement throughout the country that began in the 1880s, involving all political parties. Progressivism supported reform necessary to eliminate the abuses in various areas of our nation's life. In politics progressivism demanded an increased democratic government, giving the people a more direct voice in running their own affairs. Socially, progressivism sought a remedy for the plight of those who were poor and neglected. The most publicized effort of progressivism was the insistence that government control the large corporations and special interest groups, which seemed to be almost totally unchecked in their influence and power.

However, after World War I the country wanted to forget the causes and campaigns of progressivism and the heroes of the war. The citizens wanted to be left alone, earning a living and pursuing the happiness so well outlined in the Declaration of Independence. Wilson had added strength, dignity, and power to the office of president. His Christian character, resulting from his strong belief in the God of the Bible, had also influenced the United States in a positive way. However, the time had arrived for the nation's political leader to be more in the background, rather than up front leading the charge forward in the image made so popular by Theodore "Teddy" Roosevelt.

**Return to normalcy.** President Harding's election in 1920 as a Republican marked the beginning of a strong current of conservatism. The progressivism of the Democratic Party, marked by expanded government and strong executive leadership, was yielding to a return to the prewar state of affairs. Harding had won the election with a low-key and soft-sell approach; he proceeded with this policy that acted as a healing balm to a weary people. Although Harding was weak in certain areas of his life, the people responded to his personality warmly and enthusiastically.

National Archives

**Warren G. Harding**

Few people in the United States were upset when President Wilson's Fourteen Points to help Europe with its postwar settlements was largely rejected at home and abroad. Wilson's fourteenth point, calling for a League of Nations, was accepted in Europe, but the United States refused to join. Although strict **isolationism** was no longer possible for the people of the United States, they wanted no part of being caught up in an international organization. The nation realized the necessity of helping to solve world problems, but it wanted to avoid military involvement. This thinking permeated American foreign policy throughout the twenties, indicating that the country was protecting its self-interests in its return to normalcy.

Associated with the ending of the war was a strong movement toward **disarmament**. A Washington Disarmament Conference concerned with naval disarmament in the Pacific was called by the United States in 1921. A treaty was established among the United States, France, Britain, Italy, and Japan. This treaty provided for a ten-year ban against building new battleships or aircraft carriers, and replacements of existing ships were made subject to restrictions. However, the countries involved soon became displeased with the treaty because it had no effective enforcement power.

The *Kellogg-Briand Pact* of 1928 was an idealistic agreement by fifteen nations, including the U.S., to renounce war in settling disagreements with one another. However, the flaw in this peace pact was that it did not cover wars for self-defense, a position taken by some nations to justify wars. It also had no enforcement mechanism. Moreover, the United States esteemed the Monroe Doctrine more than this utopian agreement, thus it had little likelihood of ever being an effective international treaty.

Another strong concern during this era was the large number of immigrants who entered the United States after World War I. Many citizens in the United States were opposed to the presence of these immigrants because of their foreign appearance, customs, and speech. Working men also felt threatened that their good wages and jobs would be lost to this cheap labor market of immigrants.

In 1921 Congress passed the Emergency Quota Act, restricting the admission of foreigners to three percent per year of the number of each nationality living in the United States in 1910. After Coolidge became president, Congress enacted a new law. Under the Immigration Act of 1924, only two percent of a particular nationality residing in the United States in 1890 would be admitted each year. By establishing the quota according to the base date 1890, the law discriminated against the southern and eastern Europeans. At that time very few people from that part of Europe had settled in the United States. The 1924 law also excluded all Asiatic people. Beginning in 1927, immigration was to be limited to an annual quota of only 150,000 persons. This program of restrictive immigration was quite different from the former policy of receiving most people who wanted to enter the United States.

If the return to normalcy was to be achieved, government spending would have to be cut and taxes, especially for large businesses, would have to be decreased. A reduction in taxes and an increase in income were believed to be necessary to produce more jobs and a healthier economy. Hence, in 1921 Congress repealed the excess profits tax and lowered surtaxes on large incomes from a wartime high of 65 percent to 50 percent. This action was only the beginning of a series of tax reductions passed by Republican administrations in the 1920s. These reductions were helpful primarily to those who had large incomes.

As in several previous administrations, President Harding's administration had its share of scandals. Receiving money for pardons and illicit activities, such as liquor production and distribution, were common within the administration. The most publicized problem among discrediting events was known as the *Teapot Dome Scandal*. This scandal concerned federal conservation policies and the leasing of oil reserves that had previously been set aside by Presidents Taft and Wilson. In May of 1921 control of the oil reserves was transferred from the Navy Department to the Department of Interior headed by Albert B. Fall, one of President Harding's cabinet members and a close friend. Secretary Fall leased the Teapot Dome reserve in Wyoming to Harry F. Sinclair. Later, Fall leased the Elk Hills reserve in California to Edward L. Doheny. These transactions were done illegally without the proper public bids, and the persons involved derived a large profit from these arrangements. Secretary Fall was later convicted of receiving a bribe. He was sentenced to one year in jail and fined $100,000. However, the damage to the credibility of Harding's administration was far more costly.

## CHANGING POSTWAR LIFESTYLES

During the 1920s many people were pursuing a life of pleasure. However, although some people followed a **hedonistic** philosophy, others were concerned about creating a sound lifestyle for their families. Many people moved to urban centers to improve their lifestyle. The lifestyle of the country was also changed during this time as national restrictions on alcohol were instituted.

**Urbanization. Urbanization** was a widespread phenomenon during the decade of the twenties. Although cities had been growing steadily, people streamed from the rural areas into towns and cities during the 1920s. This movement developed so rapidly that by the end of the decade no more than 25 percent of the population still resided on farms.

Rural people were attracted to urban life for many reasons. Urban areas were centers of production for much of the wealth of our country. Cities were the source of entertainment, trends, and popular lifestyles. Communication systems such as radio were strong, popular influences on the people. Dress styles, language, social values, and customs were becoming standardized through the influence of the cities.

Urban centers also attracted large numbers of immigrants hoping to find jobs quickly to raise a family. Blacks began moving to northern cities in an effort to improve their opportunities for a higher standard of living. Black people also moved to the cities to get away from the fear and poverty most were experiencing in rural areas of the South. Many northern citizens resented this influx of dislocated people.

An organization known as the Ku Klux Klan was created in the rural United States during the Reconstruction period following the Civil War. The Klan was started in 1865 by a former Confederate general, Nathaniel B. Forrest, and was composed of white supremacists who terrorized black freedmen in an effort to deny them their civil rights—most notably the right to vote. Their methods included threatening and beating many blacks and, in some cases, they resorted to murdering black people as well as their white sympathizers. Klan terrorists kept their anonymity by wearing white robes and hoods and by striking only at night. Their efforts effectively drove blacks out of southern political life. The Klan all but disappeared after the Force Bill of 1871 was passed which gave the president the authority to use federal troops against the activities of the Klan and its members.

The KKK experienced a reawakening in 1915 under the leadership of William J. Simmons, a former Methodist minister. Most of those who joined the Klan came from the rural areas of the South, Midwest, and West. The Klan was composed of men who were anti-Catholic, anti-Jewish, and anti-Black. Its activities—which included cross-burnings, whippings, torture, and murder—were directed against these groups considered "un-American" by the Klan. After a slow beginning, the Klan reached its peak membership of about four or five million people in 1924. Klan members were frequently elected to public office and became a powerful and dangerous political force throughout the South.

Unfortunately, neither the white community nor the government protested loudly enough against these abuses toward black citizens. This lack of protest and control led to the establishment and strengthening of black organizations such as the *National Association for the Advancement of Colored People*, the *National Urban League*, and Marcus Garney's *Universal Negro Improvement Association*. These groups helped combat black stereotypes and discouraged the violence and riots of black people in Chicago, Tulsa, and other U.S. cities during the twenties.

No one special plan or organization existed that changed the situation of African-Americans in our society. They began changing their perceived image as second-class citizens in a step-by-step manner. African-Americans began to receive recognition in literature and the arts. Writers such as Walter White, Countee Cullen, Langston Hughes, Claude McKay, Jessie Redmond Fauset, and Catherine Durham had works published expressing the frustrations black people had in their efforts to establish a place for themselves in the United States. In the theater, Paul Robeson and Richard B. Harrison performed admirably. In the field of music, Noble Sissle and Eubie Blake produced musical scores, and Louis Armstrong became one of the most famous musicians of all time. Although these accomplishments and others are noteworthy, African-Americans still lacked the opportunity to perform in many areas of the country.

However, urbanization gave blacks far greater opportunities for advancement in society. The rural lifestyle reminded blacks of too many negative things; therefore, their hope for the future lay in the towns and cities.

**Prohibition.** In a nation where liquor traffic had been so widespread throughout its history, efforts to curb or halt the sale of alcohol would appear to be futile. How could such a large country with a diverse citizenry unite in an effort to establish a law against buying and selling alcohol? Most historians agree that the religious people of the United States were the driving force behind the Eighteenth Amendment. Increasing membership in Jewish synagogues and Catholic and Protestant churches totaled over forty million by 1916. Although obviously not in agreement with each other in areas of theology, each group contributed to the moral stand against liquor.

Two groups of Protestants were active in the Prohibition movement. One group consisted of conservatives and fundamentalists who believed the Bible was the ageless, inspired Word of God and that people should obey its teachings against strong drink and drunkards (Proverbs 20:1). In their view, the battle against liquor was not one against liquor itself, but against the sins it caused people to commit.

The liberals and modernists comprised the second Protestant group. This group was heavily influenced by Charles Darwin's theory of evolution. They interwove Darwin's philosophy with the Bible and produced a social application of Christ's Gospel. They excluded many biblical teachings from their gospel, such as Christ's virgin birth and physical resurrection and the fact that the Bible was God's Word. Although many people in this group would not use the term "sin," they still resisted buying and selling alcohol as a social evil. They believed that alcohol needed to be done away with as society continued its evolutionary process of improvement.

Whether all their beliefs were fully accepted or not, the spirit and thrust of these groups was contagious. The stand against sin by human social action was an issue many people were very willing to support. As the memory of the physical battles of World War I faded in people's minds, a moral battle of right versus wrong regarding liquor was just beginning for the people of the United States.

By 1916 twenty-three states had gone dry, prohibiting the sale and purchase of liquor. The long crusade of Prohibition was finally completed on January 16, 1920, when the Eighteenth Amendment to our Constitution went into effect. The Prohibition Party, the Woman's Christian Temperance Union, the Anti-Saloon League, and other Prohibition organizations celebrated the success of their hard work. Support for Prohibition was also found among reformers in both the middle-class and the upper-class.

Prohibition was effective for a few years throughout most of the United States. The consumption of alcohol was diminished, and the number of alcoholics and alcohol-related diseases was reduced. Prohibitionists achieved some other forms of success during these dry years. Many religious people were against liquor because they thought bars and saloons attracted many people who ordinarily would attend church meetings. Between 1916 and 1926, church and synagogue attendance increased by about thirteen million members. Civic and social leaders tended to voice public support of Prohibition, if for no other reason than to gain respect and popularity within the community.

By the mid-twenties, however, enforcement of the Prohibition law was breaking down. The number of government agents appointed to control illegal liquor-related crimes was insufficient for the task, and many people who opposed Prohibition did little to help authorities in their abolishment efforts. Organized crime in big cities like Chicago thrived on illegal liquor. One of the best-known racketeers was Al Capone, whose gang controlled much of the liquor trade and other illegal activities. The violence associated with racketeer-controlled liquor was a major reason for people opposed to Prohibition to argue against the ban on liquor. Gangsters and their crimes increased at such an alarming rate that citizens demanded protection by the government. The lack of manpower to meet the demand for protection contributed to the repeal of the Eighteenth Amendment.

 Many rich people abused the prohibition law in an open manner. These wealthy people used their abundant finances to make **bootlegging** profitable. Indeed, bootlegging was a way many people became rich. Poorer people found many ways of obtaining liquor; some even made their own liquor by using homemade distilleries. The increased demand for alcohol and the critical attacks of the mass media on Prohibition doomed the Eighteenth Amendment.

**Complete the vocabulary matching.**

2.1    _____ disarmament

    a. the thinking that opposes a nation's involvement in political or military affairs outside its hemisphere

2.2    _____ isolationism

    b. the pursuit of pleasure as the chief activity of life

2.3    _____ urbanization

    c. making or selling liquor illegally

2.4    _____ bootlegging

    d. the growth of city living

2.5    _____ progressivism

    e. the elimination of limitation of armed forces, military equipment or weapons of war

2.6    _____ hedonistic

    f. the movement banning the buying and selling of liquor

2.7    _____ prohibition

    g. the promotion of new and more liberal ideas and changes

**Match these items with their appropriate description.**

2.8    _____ Kellogg-Briand Pact

    a. Woodrow Wilson

2.9    _____ League of Nations' author

    b. Albert B. Fall

2.10    _____ Washington Disarmament Conference

    c. 1924 legislation restricting immigration

2.11    _____ Teapot Dome Scandal

    d. Warren Harding

2.12    _____ low-key leader

    e. 1921 meeting limiting military equipment

2.13    _____ Immigration Act

    f. 1928 agreement renouncing war

**True/False.**

2.14 _____ Progressivism was supported only by the Democratic Party.

2.15 _____ Many people thought World War I would be the last war.

2.16 _____ President Wilson led the United States into a war he was anxious to enter.

2.17 _____ The progressive movement fought various problems within the United States.

2.18 _____ Communism had taken over Russia by the year 1917.

2.19 _____ Progressiveness insisted that government control large corporations and special interest groups.

2.20 _____ By the late 1920s, about 40 percent of the people of the United States remained on farms.

2.21 _____ The Ku Klux Klan was created mainly by rural people.

2.22 _____ The Klan reached its peak population in 1924.

2.23 _____ Urbanization gave African-Americans far greater opportunities for advancement.

2.24 _____ The Eighteenth Amendment prohibited the buying and selling of liquor.

2.25 _____ The Eighteenth Amendment was supported by the religious community except for Protestants.

2.26 _____ Conservatives and modernists believed the Bible to be totally true.

2.27 _____ Liberals do not necessarily believe the entire Bible is true.

**Identity the following items by matching them with their definition.**

2.28 _____ Nathaniel B. Forrest        a. started the original Ku Klux Klan

2.29 _____ Louis Armstrong             b. expansion from country living to city living

2.30 _____ urbanization                c. one of the most famous musicians of all time

2.31 _____ 1865                        d. made up largely of rural, white supremacist Americans

2.32 _____ Ku Klux Klan                e. beginning of Ku Klux Klan

2.33 _____ 1924                        f. The Immigration Act

# HISTORY & GEOGRAPHY

1 1 0 7

## LIFEPAC TEST

88 / 110

**Name**_____

**Date** _____

**Score** _____

**Match these items** (each answer, 2 points).

| | | |
|---|---|---|
| 1. | _____ New Deal | a. organization for black persons' rights |
| 2. | _____ just peace | b. legislation for veteran bonuses |
| 3. | _____ return to normalcy | c. program of flood control and soil conservation |
| 4. | _____ National Industrial Recovery Act | d. Harding's postwar program |
| 5. | _____ progressivism | e. Roosevelt's recovery program |
| 6. | _____ Tennessee Valley Authority | f. legislation controlling corporation competition practices |
| 7. | _____ Washington Disarmament Conference | g. resulted in five-nation treaty banning build-up of certain military equipment |
| 8. | _____ Patman Bill | h. Roosevelt's initial program to pass as much legislation as possible |
| 9. | _____ First Hundred Days | i. British ship sunk by Germans |
| 10. | _____ Young Plan | j. financial aid to Europe |
| 11. | _____ National Urban League | k. program of political and social reforms throughout the nation |
| 12. | _____ *Lusitania* | l. fair treatment of all nations following World War I |

**Fill in the blanks** (each answer, 3 points).

13. World peace following World War I was proposed by Wilson's _____ .

14. General _____ was commander of American forces during World War I.

15. The signing of the _____ ended World War I.

16. Wilson's organization for settling world problems was the _____ .

17. The mass movement of people to the cities is called _____ .

18. The drive to control large corporations and special interest groups beginning in the 1880s was called _____ .

19. Active involvement in world affairs is called _____ .

20. The non-involvement in world affairs is called _____ .

21. The ban on liquor sales as outlined in the Eighteenth Amendment was called _____ .

22. An organization that sought to prevent any establishment of the rights of blacks was the _____ .

**True/False** (each answer, 1 point).

23. _____ The sinking of the *Lusitania* and similar incidents drew the United States into World War I.

24. _____ The collapse of the German allies led to the German surrender in World War I.

25. _____ German land was divided and its military was reduced by the Treaty of Versailles.

26. _____ Harding's progressivism faded as the people wanted to return to a normal life after World War I.

27. _____ Frequent scandals during the Harding years damaged his credibility.

28. _____ Coolidge backed immigration restrictions and tax reductions.

29. _____ Much of the blame for the Great Depression was placed unfairly on Hoover.

30. _____ Roosevelt's policies were greatly influenced by Woodrow Wilson and Theodore Roosevelt.

31. _____ Roosevelt's determination did much to bring hope to the United States during the Great Depression.

32. _____ Stalin used dictatorial methods in Russia.

**Match these men with the items associated with them** (each letter, 2 points).

33. _____ Woodrow Wilson

34. _____ Franklin D. Roosevelt

35. _____ Herbert Hoover

36. _____ Warren G. Harding

37. _____ Calvin Coolidge

a.  Home Loan Bank System
b.  McNary-Haugen Farm Relief Bill
c.  Fourteen Points
d.  Young Plan
e.  Treaty of Versailles
f.  Civilian Conservation Corps
g.  Patman Bill
h.  Social Security Act
i.  Agricultural Adjustment Act
j.  National Industrial Recovery Act
k.  Emergency Quota Act
l.  Washington Disarmament Conference
m. Teapot Dome Scandal

**Choose the best answer(s)** (each answer, 2 points).

38.     Causes of the Great Depression included: _____ , _____ , _____ , _____

       a.  a weak national economy
       b.  agricultural overproduction
       c.  exports supported by loans
       d.  stock market stability
       e.  overextended credit

39.     A nation that was not an Allied Power of World War I was: _____ .

       a.  Britain
       b.  Japan
       c.  United States
       d.  Switzerland
       e.  France
       f.  Italy

40.     An event leading to German surrender was: _____ .

       a.  the victory of Turkey and Bulgaria
       b.  the uniting of Austria-Hungary
       c.  the United States joining the Allies
       d.  the Allies retreating from the Germans
       e.  the surrender of Russia

41.     A movement of change in the postwar United States was: _____ .

       a.  a return to a normal state of affairs
       b.  rural living
       c.  the backing of the League of Nations
       d.  the lack of Prohibition
       e.  open immigration

42.     Legislation passed during Harding's administration was the: _____ .

       a.  Armament Race Bill
       b.  Eighteenth Amendment
       c.  Teapot Dome Scandal
       d.  Prohibition Act
       e.  Emergency Quota Act

**Answer the following question** (each answer, 4 points).

43.     How did Roosevelt's background prepare him for the difficulties of the depression years?

_____

_____

_____

_____

**Choose the best answer(s).**

2.34    Which two factors caused the enforcement of the Eighteenth Amendment to break down?
　　　　____    a.   lack of government agents to control illegal liquor-related crimes
　　　　____    b.   people opposing Prohibition did little to help authorities
　　　　____    c.   too many alcohol related diseases
　　　　____    d.   support among reformers in both middle-class and the upper-class

**Answer the following question.**

2.35    What were the advantages and disadvantages of the Eighteenth Amendment?

_____

_____

_____

_____

_____

_____

_____

_____

**Adult Check**    _____
　　　　　　　　　　　　**Initial**　　　　**Date**

Review the material in this section in preparation for the Self Test. This Self Test will check your mastery of this particular section as well as your knowledge of the previous section.

# SELF TEST 2

**Identify the following items by matching them with their descriptions** (each answer, 2 points).

2.01 _____ Eighteenth Amendment

a. agreement of fifteen nations to renounce war

2.02 _____ Ku Klux Klan

b. led to the U.S. involvement in World War I

2.03 _____ Kellogg-Briand Pact

c. given back to France after World War I

2.04 _____ Washington Disarmament Conference

d. banned the buying and selling of liquor in the U.S.

2.05 _____ Teapot Dome Scandal

e. Wilson's policy of political and social reform in the United States

2.06 _____ Treaty of Versailles

f. organization promoting African-American rights

2.07 _____ Alsace-Lorraine

g. scandal concerning oil reserves

2.08 _____ *Lusitania*

h. peace treaty at the end of World War I

2.09 _____ National Urban League

i. five-nation treaty limiting or banning certain military equipment

2.010 _____ progressivism

j. organization known for its anti-black measures

**Match these items with their descriptions** (each answer, 2 points).

2.011 _____ Pershing

a. mass movement to the cities

2.012 _____ Ferdinand

b. ban of liquor sales

2.013 _____ Versailles

c. involvement in world affairs

2.014 _____ Wilson

d. Wilson's peace proposal

2.015 _____ Harding

e. Austrian Archduke who was assassinated

2.016 _____ urbanization

f. site for signing of World War I peace treaty

2.017 _____ prohibition

g. president returning the United States to normalcy

2.018 _____ isolationism

h. president supporting progressivism

2.019 _____ internationalism

i. commander of American forces during World War I

2.020 _____ Fourteen Points

j. organization for peaceful settlement of world problems

2.021 _____ League of Nations

k. separation from world affairs

**True/False** (each answer, 1 point).

2.022   _____ Austrian-Serbian hostilities initiated World War I.

2.023   _____ Britain entered World War I when Germany defied Serbian neutrality.

2.024   _____ The American reinforcements prevented the massive German offensive in northeastern France from being successful.

2.025   _____ Advocates of a just peace won out at the Paris peace talks.

2.026   _____ The United States wanted a change from Wilson's progressivism after World War I.

2.027   _____ The United States rejected the League of Nations because of U.S. policies of internationalism.

2.028   _____ Many scandals brought suspicions concerning Harding's credibility.

2.029   _____ The United States began a program of restrictive immigration during the 1920s.

2.030   _____ Prohibition was backed by many groups of the United States' religious community.

2.031   _____ Urbanization gave black people hope of better opportunities and advancement.

**Choose the best answer and write the letter on the line** (each answer, 2 points).

2.032   A nation that was *not* an Allied Power of World War I was: \_\_\_\_\_ .
    a. Britain
    b. Japan
    c. United States
    d. Switzerland
    e. France
    f. Italy

2.033   An event leading to German surrender was: \_\_\_\_\_ .
    a. the victory of Turkey and Bulgaria
    b. the uniting of Austria-Hungary
    c. the United States joining the Allies
    d. the Allies retreating from the Germans
    e. the surrender of Russia

2.034   A movement of change in the postwar United States was: \_\_\_\_\_ .
    a. a return to a normal state of affairs
    b. rural living
    c. the backing of the League of Nations
    d. the lack of Prohibition
    e. open immigration

2.035   Legislation passed during Harding's administration was the: \_\_\_\_\_ .
    a. Armament Race Bill
    b. Eighteenth Amendment
    c. Teapot Dome Scandal
    d. Prohibition Act
    e. Emergency Quota Act

2.036     A factor that did *not* attract people to city living was: _____ .
          a.  hope for monetary gains
          b.  opportunities for advancement
          c.  available jobs
          d.  vigilantism

2.037     One group *not* in favor of Prohibition was: _____ .
          a.  Protestant fundamentalists
          b.  Catholics
          c.  liberals and modernists
          d.  bootleggers
          e.  Jewish community

2.038     What caused the United States to break its neutrality and enter World War I? _____
          a.  the assassination of Ferdinand
          b.  the constant German sinking of trading vessels resulting in loss of lives
          c.  the German march across Bulgaria
          d.  the surrender of Turkey and Bulgaria

**Fill in the blank** (each answer, 2 points).

2.039     One of the negative effects of Prohibition was a rise in _____ .

**Answer the following question** (each answer, 4 points).

2.040     Why did President Harding develop a program to return to normalcy?

          _____

          _____

          _____

          _____

          _____

          _____

          _____

58 / 72

Score
Adult Check     _____
                _____
                **Initial        Date**

28

# III. THE GREAT DEPRESSION

The period of the 1920s was one of achievement and prosperity. The Coolidge administration was responsive to the will of the majority of the citizens and strengthened the nation's economy by reducing unemployment and taxes. Although disagreements arose concerning the nation's role overseas, the people were united in their efforts after the war to restore the United States first. Consequently, business and industry boomed. The sudden collapse into economic depression from a position of apparent economic prosperity devastated the nation's work force and morale. In this section you will study the economic conditions that existed before and during the Great Depression and the effects the depression had on both rich and poor citizens.

## SECTION OBJECTIVES

**Review these objectives.** When you have completed this section, you should be able to:

6. Outline the philosophy and policies of Coolidge:

   6.1 List the major programs and concerns of Coolidge.

   6.2 Describe the struggle between internationalism and isolationism in the United States.

7. Describe the prosperity and disaster of the Hoover years:

   7.1 Describe the surface prosperity of the United States in the 1920s.

   7.2 List the factors leading to our nation's unhealthy economic condition.

8. Describe the effects of the Great Depression on the United States' wealthy and poor.

## VOCABULARY

**Study these words** to enhance your learning success in this section.

| | |
|---|---|
| **foreclosure** | The act of taking away ownership of land when a debt on it cannot be paid |
| **internationalism** | The thinking that a nation should be actively involved in world affairs |
| **speculative** | Given to theorizing or taking a chance |

# PROGRESS BEFORE THE DEPRESSION

Outwardly, the economy of the United States in the 1920s never seemed better. Production rates were increasing, and the public enjoyed a prosperous life. However, strong underlying defects indicated an unhealthy economic condition. The leadership of the United States throughout these productive but shattering years was entrusted to Calvin Coolidge and Herbert Hoover.

**The Coolidge years.** Like Harding, Calvin Coolidge did not provide the country with strong executive leadership. The power and prestige of the presidency, which had grown so strong under Theodore Roosevelt and Woodrow Wilson, was reduced when Coolidge took office following Harding's death.

President Calvin Coolidge was born in 1872 in Vermont. He came from a hard-working family, and after graduating from Amherst College and law school, he entered private law practice. He became lieutenant governor and later governor of Massachusetts. Coolidge was not very outgoing—he was very careful in his relationships with people in both private and public life. He talked so little that he became known as "Silent Cal."

**Calvin Coolidge**

President Coolidge was a hard working, moral, frugal, and dedicated president. As a political conservative, he was in agreement with Harding's philosophy regarding normalcy. Although not totally insensitive to rural areas, he strongly believed that what was best for industry was best for the United States. The scandals of Harding's administration were soon ameliorated by Coolidge's stern stand for morality. Coolidge backed immigration restrictions, tax reduction, and bonuses for World War I veterans. Coolidge's administrative policies were following the desires of the majority of the people in the United States.

Coolidge did not personally campaign for election in 1924. Charles G. Dawes, the Republican vice presidential nominee handled that assignment quite well. With the campaign slogan of "Keep Cool with Coolidge," the Republicans scored an overwhelming victory. The results reinforced Coolidge's plan to continue Harding's policies.

However, Coolidge soon had to deal with the question of farm relief. Agriculture was in trouble from overproduction and low prices in the 1920s. Midwestern farmers pushed legislation known as the McNary-Haugen Farm Relief Bill, challenging the president and the federal government to raise farm prices. Although many farmers were Republicans, Coolidge vetoed that bill twice during his term in office. Many farmers were alienated when the president insisted that they solve their own problems.

Coolidge fared better with tax reduction with the help of his secretary of the treasury, Andrew W. Mellon. Secretary Mellon's contention was that a lowered tax structure "increases the amount of capital which is put into production enterprises, stimulates business, and makes more certain that more $5,000 jobs will be available to go around." The unemployment rate was also directly related to the tax structure. This relationship is quite impressive in the light of a national budget surplus throughout the 1920s.

Much of the budget surplus accumulated by limiting new government programs and cutting others. From 1923 to 1929, the national debt was cut to $16 billion after being $24 billion in 1920. President Coolidge explained this phenomenon in a speech to Congress in 1928:

> Four times we have made a drastic revision of our internal revenue system, abolishing many taxes and substantially reducing almost all others. Each time the resulting stimulation to business has so increased taxable incomes and profits that a surplus has been produced.

Although this statement may have been slightly inflated in praising the benefits of his tax laws, Coolidge did have reason to justify his policy—the nation was having a business boom.

By the mid-1920s, **internationalism** and isolationism were of great concern to the people of the United States. Proponents of internationalism believed that the interests of the United States were universal. The internationalists insisted that the United States should be concerned about any place on earth where people were persecuted or endangered. Isolationism theorists, on the other hand, resisted the political or military involvement of the United States outside of the Western Hemisphere. The internationalists wanted the United States to play an important role in world affairs, but the isolationists strongly resented any such participation.

Americans tended to be more flexible in the practical area of world commerce than the theories of either isolationism or internationalism allowed. The position taken by the country was that involvement did not constitute commitment. This position worked well as our nation strove to maintain peace. Adherents of both sides subscribed to the slogan of "America first." This unity was a healthy sign for a country with varying beliefs.

In an effort to help Europe with its financial troubles, the United States cooperated in forming the Young Plan, named after American businessman Owen D. Young. The Young Plan reduced German reparations from $33 billion to $9 billion, giving hope that this reduction would help Germany to pay its international war debts. The United States also invested large amounts of money in Germany's industry, helping Germany to prosper enough to begin payments to other European countries. These European countries then made payments to the United States for wartime debts.

Apparently, the United States was not taking isolationism seriously at the government and business levels. With so much trade and capital going into Asia, Latin America, and Europe, the true picture of United States isolationism is not difficult to perceive.

When he addressed the Connecticut Chamber of Commerce in May of 1925, Curtis Wilbur, secretary of the navy under Coolidge, stated, "Americans have over twenty million tons of merchant shipping to carry the commerce of the world, worth three billion dollars. We have laws and property abroad, exclusive of government loans, of over ten billions of dollars…These vast interests must be defended unhesitatingly and with all our power whenever attacked…To defend America we must be prepared to defend its interests and our flag in every corner of the globe." Anyone hearing the speech could envision the United States moving toward increased global involvement.

Although it was a defeated country, Germany remained potentially the most powerful nation in Europe. The determination of the Germans had not been broken, and they still had the desire to dominate Western Europe. Also during the 1920s, Russia was under the ruthless domination of Joseph Stalin. Stalin assumed the leadership of the Russians after the death of Lenin, the man who inspired the Russian Revolution in 1917. Stalin expounded Karl Marx's philosophy that the capitalism of Western society was mankind's enemy. This threatening philosophy, together with Germany's potential, became a concern to the United States when the weak positions of France and Great Britain were considered. Without United States support, France and Great Britain could not keep the Russian or German armies from moving quickly across Europe.

An area of United States intervention that did not receive much publicity was Latin America. Although encouraging self-determination in many countries, the United States was protecting its own interests by militarily occupying Latin American countries such as Santo Domingo, Haiti, and Nicaragua. In 1928 a State Department officer, J. Reuben Clark, released his memorandum on the Monroe Doctrine. Mr. Clark insisted that previous American involvement in Latin American affairs sought only to guarantee hemispheric "freedom, independence, and territorial integrity against the imperialistic designs of Europe." However, a respected mutual relationship was accepted by Latin America only after the implementation of President Roosevelt's Good Neighbor Policy.

Coolidge's popularity remained strong throughout his term of office. His differences with farmers had eased because of an increase in rural farm prosperity. Many people agreed with President Coolidge when he told Congress in his last annual message in December 1928, "The country can regard the present with satisfaction and anticipate the future with optimism." A *New York Times* editorial stated that Coolidge had "fitted exactly into the needs and inarticulate desires of the American people when he became president."

When President Coolidge finished his term of office, the people of the United States were confident and optimistic about the future. However, few people expected that Coolidge's reply to re-election talk would be so famous. His answer was simply, "I do not choose to run." The wisdom and timing of this decision would be indelibly marked in the minds of United States citizens.

National Archives

**Herbert Hoover**

**The Hoover years.** Herbert Hoover became president in the spring of 1929 under extremely good economic conditions. In his inaugural address he stated, "Ours is a land rich in resources; stimulating in its glorious beauty; filled with millions of happy homes; blessed with comfort and opportunity. In no nation are the fruits of accomplishment more secure."

Mr. Hoover was born in 1874 in West Branch, Iowa and attended Stanford University. After his graduation, Hoover accepted a position working for a British mining company that allowed him to travel around the world. By 1914 the future president was quite wealthy and embarked on a new career as a public servant—he served as secretary of commerce under Presidents Harding and Coolidge. Unfortunately for Mr. Hoover, his background did not adequately prepare him for what he was about to face. National circumstances were such that Hoover's name became so resented that it was used primarily in a mocking or derogatory sense.

Shortly after Charles Mitchell (Chairman of the National City Bank of New York) stated that "the industrial situation of the United States is absolutely sound," the stock market collapsed. The nation was not prepared for such a shock; thousands of people were bankrupt. Mr. Mitchell's opinion was one with which many people agreed in October 1929; no reason existed to think otherwise. Between 1923 and 1929 the United States enjoyed one of the most prosperous periods in its history. Goods were being produced at a rapid rate as millions of citizens bought new automobiles, houses, and modern conveniences.

Although the United States still had poor people, no other nation on earth could boast of so much prosperity and achievement. Hoover may have been exaggerating when he said at his presidential nomination in 1928, "We in America today are nearer to the final triumph over poverty than ever before in the history of any land." These words were based on an extremely successful economy and a prosperous citizenry. His remark was followed by a statement issued from the Committee on Recent Economic Changes, reported in 1929, that "never before has the human race made such progress in solving the problem of production."

The nation's economy seemed healthy in the late twenties, especially if one looked at the growth of industry. The main cause of this rapid growth was the production of motor vehicles. Between 1920 and 1929 the annual sales of automobiles, trucks, and buses jumped from 2,227,000 to 5,337,000. The mass production assembly lines kept prices at figures most families could afford. The popularity of the automobile led to tremendous growth of another industry—oil. The Greater Seminole oil field was discovered in 1926, and the Oklahoma City oil field was discovered two years later. Both provided plenty of oil for the nation's use. Construction also flourished during the 1920s. Hundreds of thousands of new homes were built for returning veterans of World War I and for many who sought a suburban lifestyle. Jobs were plentiful, and wages kept up with the cost of living. Wages continued to rise, and working hours steadily decreased before 1929.

The unionization of labor was well underway by the 1920s. Private companies strongly resented unions and fought hard to keep them out of their businesses. Most union members were affiliated with the American Federation of Labor, an organization representing many skilled crafts. The unions stated that they stood for employee benefits such as better wages, shorter working hours, and improved working conditions. However, companies stated that they themselves would improve the employee's situation without the help of unions. Some businesses organized their own company unions in an effort to combat the larger union movement.

**Match these vocabulary words with their definitions.**

3.1 _____ internationalism

3.2 _____ speculativ

3.3 _____ foreclosure

a. the act of taking away land for a debt

b. the thinking that a nation should be actively involved in world affairs

c. given to theorizing or taking a chance


**Match the following.**

3.4 _____ Coolidge

3.5 _____ Dawes

3.6 _____ McNary-Haugen Bills

3.7 _____ Mellon

3.8 _____ internationalism

3.9 _____ isolationism

3.10 _____ Young Plan

3.11 _____ Marx

3.12 _____ Stalin

3.13 _____ Lenin

a. American interests should be universal

b. originated philosophy that Western capitalism was the enemy of mankind

c. inspired the Russian Revolution of 1917

d. managed Coolidge's presidential campaign

e. legislation to raise farm prices

f. non-involvement in world affairs

g. Russian ruler who used dictatorial methods

h. legislation to help Europe with its financial troubles

i. president favoring tax reduction


**Fill in the blanks.**

3.14 Herbert Hoover attended _____ University.

3.15 Hoover served as _____ under Presidents Harding and Coolidge.

3.16 Two large oil fields that were discovered in the 1920s were the _____ field and the _____ field.

3.17 By the 1920s, most union members were affiliated with the _____ .

Although very favorable economic conditions existed in the twenties, major defects quickly appeared. Some large industries were never as successful as they tried to appear. When the stock market crashed, the nation's troubled economy was shown to be very weak. Agriculture was the primary area of the country's economy that gave an indication of troubled times ahead. With advanced machinery, better quality seeds, and increased efficiency, farmers should have been very prosperous. Unfortunately, these farmers were producing more than they could sell. Because of such an abundance of food, prices continued to fall, thus lowering profits. Competition from foreign countries, especially Canada and Australia, further complicated matters. After President Hoover was elected, federally funded programs were adapted to alleviate the plight of United States agriculture. Unfortunately, these programs lost millions of dollars for the government because of the depression.

The United States' foreign trade program provided another indication of the nation's unhealthy economic condition. Although foreign exports exceeded imports, loans to foreign countries were used to buy goods from the United States. In a sense, the people in the United States were paying for their own exports. This practice was extremely dangerous and depended on continually loaning money to foreign countries to maintain exports.

The problem of credit also arose. Many citizens who could not afford the farm and factory products resorted to buying on credit. Yet without available credit, customer purchases would be cut, and products would go unsold and be stockpiled. A decrease in customer purchases would cause heavy unemployment. As prosperity in the United States continued to rise in the late 1920s, economists were becoming more aware that the prosperity was artificial. Stock prices increased with **speculative** buying rather than with substantive investment.

President Hoover's words to the nation on October 25, 1929, were that "the fundamental business of the country, that is, production and distribution of commodities, is on a sound and prosperous basis." Robert P. Lamont, secretary of commerce, also indicated that none of the underlying factors that had been associated with or had preceded the decline in business in the past were then in existence. William Green, president of the American Federation of Labor (AF of L) expressed the view that "within a few months we will be back to a normal state in the industrial and economic life of the nation." However, these assurances did not prevent the coming of the Great Depression.

**Headlines from the *New York Times* on October 29, 1929**

A decade of overproduction, vastly overextended credit, uncontrolled spending, and a get-rich-quick philosophy ended very abruptly. On October 24, 1929, excessive selling dropped prices to dangerous levels. Disaster struck on October 29, 1929, when frantic stockholders offered 16,410,000 shares for sale at almost giveaway prices. Some stocks could not be sold at any price. The sudden collapse of the stock market caused hundreds of thousands of stockholders to become bankrupt. The stock market crash greatly affected the financial community, particularly Wall Street, and marked the start of the worst economic depression in the history of the United States.

To combat what was happening, President Hoover called for a series of White House meetings to urge businessmen to maintain wage rates and employment. Labor was cautioned to avoid wage increases. The president requested an increase in federal public works and asked governors to enlarge state-supported projects. In December of 1929, Congress reduced both corporate and individual income taxes.

Many people commended the president's actions. On December 1 the *New York Times* wrote, "Too much praise cannot be given the president for the prompt and resolute and skillful way in which he set about reassuring the country after the financial collapse." Despite some feeling of optimism, by 1930 people could clearly see the effects of the depression. Four million people were already jobless. President Hoover pleaded for private business and industry to help in whatever way they could. Local and state officials were encouraged to support the needy people in their areas. However, this plea was difficult to carry out because of the overwhelming demands from the destitute citizens. President Hoover strongly resisted the appeals for more federal funds. He was firmly convinced that the private sector of the country would rise to the occasion and meet the crisis.

## CONDITIONS DURING THE DEPRESSION

During the twenties a large gap existed between high and low levels of incomes in the United States. This unevenness of finances caused problems for the nation's economy. The rich attempted to get richer, and the poor only managed to survive.

**Outlook for the rich.** By 1929, 40 percent of the country's total income was derived from the families in the top 10 percent financially. This elite group purchased the normal consumer goods, but they also indulged in risky speculative investments, hoping to get even richer as quickly as possible. Much of their money went into the stock market and was later lost. Some individuals became poor literally overnight. However, others within this group had enough wealth stored up to absorb the loss and to suffer some inconveniences without going bankrupt.

The depression was not necessarily the fault of our nation's wealthy people, who caused bitter and even radical talk. This talk showed the frustration many people had toward the nation's economic system. Resentment arose easily in a country that had storehouses of wheat not being used while children were going hungry. People went without clothing while warehouses remained full of surplus cotton. British economist John Maynard Keynes wrote in 1932 that the depression was "not a crisis of poverty, but a crisis of abundance." The problem was getting this abundance to the needy.

Although many workers were laid off, business executives maintained their positions. Owners of small companies performed the menial tasks they had previously paid others to do. Large automobile corporations, such as Ford, Chrysler, and General Motors, had made such huge profits during the 1920s that the cutbacks of the depression only curtailed large increases in profits; many executive employees were secure in their jobs throughout the depression years. Other relatively secure employment was found in newspaper publishing companies, tobacco companies, and private utility companies. Having a job during the years immediately following 1929 made one comparatively prosperous.

**Plight of the poor.** The nation's jobless people lined up by the millions for unemployment relief. Public kitchens operated in many urban areas to distribute soup, bread, and other food to starving families. Some people with money bought boxes of apples to sell on the street. The most menial jobs would be taken as soon as they were available. People lost farms, homes, and other property through **foreclosure** proceedings. Many people in the United States were beginning to experience a sense of hopelessness.

During the summer of 1932, World War I veterans showed their frustration by marching on Washington. This public display was a demand for the payment of war bonuses voted to them by Congress in 1924. *The Patman Bill*, passed by the House of Representatives, called for the payment of the remaining bonus money. When the Senate voted the bill down, thousands of veterans remained in Washington and demonstrated against the decision. Riots broke out against the police, and federal troops led by General Douglas MacArthur were called in to remove the veterans.

Also during the summer of 1932, farmers in the Midwest demanded that prices of their products be raised. Milo Reno led a group of angry farmers to form the *National Farmers' Holiday Association* at Des Moines, Iowa. This association began strikes in the Midwest and even blocked the efforts of other farmers trying to get their milk and livestock to market. By 1933 farm prices were still declining. Agricultural income was only one-third of what it was in 1929. Wheat could be bought for twenty-five cents a bushel; before the depression it sold for one dollar a bushel. Cotton prices fell almost as drastically.

Unemployment rose from 4 million in 1930 to over 12 million by 1933; approximately one-fourth of the labor force in the United States was out of work. Unfortunately, the private sector of our nation did not "rise to the occasion" as President Hoover had hoped. Some families lived on two or three dollars a week for food, and many rural families had no money at all.

**Faces of the Depression**

In March of 1932, Hoover grudgingly approved Congress' distribution of 40 million bushels of wheat and 5 million bales of cotton. The president insisted that the Red Cross distribute these products and others, keeping with his stand that the federal government would not engage in actual distribution of relief. However, in June of 1932, Hoover approved a loan from the Reconstruction Finance Corporation of 300 million dollars for direct relief. One hundred million dollars also was provided for rediscount banks that gave credit to banks and financial institutions. In July of 1932, Congress provided for the creation of a Home Loan Bank System to help owners who were about to lose their homes. Although these measures were helpful and appeased some people, more federal funds were needed to attack the depression. More than two thousand banks closed their doors in 1931; billions of dollars in deposits were lost. The situation of the nation was desperate.

**True/False.**

3.18 _____ The stock market crash showed the weakness of our nation's economy.

3.19 _____ Foreign trade was healthy before the depression.

3.20 _____ The stock market collapsed on October 29, 1929.

3.21 _____ The stock market crash only affected stockholders and brokers.

**Choose the best answers.**

3.22 What were three major things that led to the stock market crash?
_____ a. overextended credit
_____ b. not enough product production
_____ c. uncontrolled spending
_____ d. overproduction
_____ e. massive foreclosures
_____ f. prosperity

3.23 What were three groups other than automobile corporations that were financially well-off during the depression?
_____ a. clothing manufacturers
_____ b. newspaper publishers
_____ c. oil companies
_____ d. private utility companies
_____ e. tobacco companies

**Match these items with the appropriate description.**

3.24 _____ Patman Bill                              a. led federal troops to stop veteran riots

3.25 _____ MacArthur                               b. direct relief for people in need

3.26 _____ Reno                                    c. legislation for bonus money for veterans

3.27 _____ Reconstruction Finance Corporation      d. led farmers to form the National farmers' Holiday Association

3.28 _____ Home Loan Bank System                   e. financial aid for homeowners

**Answer the following question.**

3.29    What was the situation of the large automobile corporations during the depression?

_____
_____
_____
_____
_____
_____
_____

**Adult Check**    _____
                    **Initial**        **Date**


3.30    What measures did Hoover take when the private sector of the nation did not "rise to the occasion"?

_____
_____
_____
_____
_____
_____
_____

**Adult Check**    _____
                    **Initial**        **Date**

 Review the material in this section in preparation for the Self Test. This Self Test will check your mastery of this particular section as well as your knowledge of the previous sections.

# SELF TEST 3

**Fill in the blanks** (each answer, 3 points).

3.01    The popularity of President _____'s progressivism faded after World War I.

3.02    The presidential campaign for Calvin Coolidge was led by _____.

3.03    President _____'s program for a return to normalcy was backed by the people of the United States.

3.04    The philosophy that Western capitalism was the enemy of mankind was started by _____.

3.05    A nation's involvement in world affairs is called _____.

3.06    The dictatorial Russian leader who took power after Lenin was _____.

3.07    The non-involvement of a nation in world affairs is called _____.

3.08    The mass movement of rural people to the city is called _____.

3.09    The _____ put prohibition laws into effect.

3.010   The signing of the _____ by the Germans brought peace at the end of World War I.

3.011   President Hoover's main weakness in dealing with the depression was that he trusted the _____ too much.


**True/False** (each answer, 1 point).

3.012   _____ The sinking of the *Lusitania* and similar incidents resulting in American deaths led the United States into World War I.

3.013   _____ The United States struggled between policies of internationalism and isolationism during the twenties.

3.014   _____ High wages and better opportunities drove many to move to the cities of the United States.

3.015   _____ Foreign trade was unhealthy just before the depression because American loans were paying for American exports.

3.016   _____ Most people in the United States were not expecting the stock market to crash.

3.017   _____ Coolidge declined to run for reelection because of his loss of popularity among the people.

3.018   _____ The depression left many business executives jobless.

**Match these items** (each answer, 2 points).

| | | | |
|---|---|---|---|
| 3.019 | _____ | McNary-Haugen Farm Relief Bill | a. financial legislation to aid Europe |
| 3.020 | _____ | Young Plan | b. organization promoting rights of black people |
| 3.021 | _____ | American Federation of Labor | c. financial aid for homeowners |
| 3.022 | _____ | Patman Bill | d. legislation for bonus money to veterans |
| 3.023 | _____ | National Farmers' Holiday Association | e. legislation to raise farm prices |
| 3.024 | _____ | Reconstruction Finance Corporation | f. agreement by fifteen nations to renounce war |
| 3.025 | _____ | Home Loan Bank System | g. Hoover's direct relief for people in need |
| 3.026 | _____ | Kellogg-Briand Pact | h. organization preventing rights of black people |
| 3.027 | _____ | Ku Klux Klan | i. labor union for employee benefits |
| 3.028 | _____ | National Urban League | j. organization striking for raise in farm prices |

**Choose the best answer(s)** (each answer, 2 points).

3.029    Five postwar movements of change in the United States were:

_____ a. a return to normalcy
_____ b. Prohibition
_____ c. urbanization
_____ d. restrictive immigration
_____ e. tax increases
_____ f. disarmament

3.030    Four measures backed by the Coolidge administration were:

_____ a. immigration restriction
_____ b. raising in farm prices
_____ c. tax reduction
_____ d. veteran bonuses
_____ e. a stand for morality

3.031    Four causes of the Great Depression were:

_____ a. a weak national economy
_____ b. agricultural overproduction
_____ c. an imbalance of foreign trade
_____ d. stock market stability
_____ e. overextended credit

3.032    Three measures taken by President Hoover to combat the depression were:

_____    a.  the National Farmers' Holiday Association

_____    b.  the Reconstruction Finance Corporation

_____    c.  a plea to the private sector

_____    d.  the Home Loan Bank System

3.033    Mark three factors that drew rural people to the cities.

_____    a.  higher wages, or money

_____    b.  to join the Ku Klux Klan

_____    c.  greater opportunities for advancement in society

_____    d.  cities were centers of entertainment, trends, and popular lifestyles

_____    e.  to defend traditional values and ideas

78 / 98

Score
Adult Check

_____

_____
Initial          Date

---

# IV. THE NEW DEAL

When the 1930s began, the American economy was extremely depressed, and the morale of the nation was very low. President Hoover's efforts and optimistic statements had not been completely successful. Although many blamed Hoover for much of the Great Depression, it was not his fault. However, new and able leadership was desperately needed to guide the United States through that time of hopelessness and despair. Franklin D. Roosevelt provided the necessary leadership. He came to the presidency with a background that uniquely prepared him to meet the challenge of the time; he also had a plan to bring the country and its people to a position of prosperity.

## SECTION OBJECTIVES

**Review these objectives.** When you have completed this section, you should be able to:

9.   Explain the effects of Franklin D. Roosevelt's leadership on recovery in the United States during the depression years:

9.1   Explain how Roosevelt's background prepared him for the job of rescuing the United States from the Great Depression.

9.2   Describe Roosevelt's philosophy of recovery.

9.3   Explain the promises and plans Roosevelt put into action for the nation's recovery.

# VOCABULARY

Study these words to enhance your learning success in this section.

| | |
|---|---|
| **apropos** | Suited to the time, place, or occasion |
| **collective bargaining** | Negotiation between organized workers and employers on wages, hours, conditions, and benefits |
| **sharecropper** | A tenant farmer who pays a share of his crop as rent for his land |

## THE FOUNDER OF THE NEW DEAL

The famed saying, "Now is the time for all good men to come to the aid of their country" was never more **apropos** than during the early thirties. Franklin Delano Roosevelt was very well prepared for the job. His political career gave him valuable experience and helped him to function with great confidence and efficiency as president of the United States.

**Franklin D. Roosevelt**

**His personal preparation.** Being a distant cousin of former President Theodore Roosevelt gave Franklin Roosevelt's name an image that commanded respect. His father, James Roosevelt, was a wealthy railroad man. Franklin Roosevelt had private tutors until he was fourteen years old. He spent a great deal of time in outdoor activities such as fishing, bird-watching, and livestock farming. Two of his hobbies were collecting model ships and collecting stamps. Roosevelt's outgoing personality and inner confidence continued to grow through his careful training during his childhood in Hyde Park, New York.

After graduating from Groton School in Massachusetts, young Franklin entered Harvard University where he spent four productive years. Roosevelt was editor of the school's newspaper, an experience that served him well during his political career. After Harvard, Roosevelt graduated from Columbia University Law School in 1907 and began private practice with a law firm in New York.

The future president was elected as a Democratic state senator in New York in 1910 and was reelected in 1912. He served as assistant secretary of the navy from 1913 to 1921 under President Wilson. In 1920 Roosevelt ran for vice president on a Democratic ticket with James M. Cox, the governor of Ohio. However, the Republican candidate, Warren G. Harding, won the election by a landslide, and Franklin Roosevelt returned to private law practice in New York.

In the summer of 1921 Roosevelt contracted polio. His legs were almost completely paralyzed, but he refused to be defeated by the disease. An indication of his determination can be seen in his statement, "Once I spent two years in bed trying to move my big toe; after that job anything seems easy."

Franklin Roosevelt was elected governor of New York in 1928 in a political comeback. As governor he wrestled with problems at the state level similar to those that Hoover encountered at the national level. In 1930 he started a broad relief program in New York that set a pattern he could later use for the entire country. The name of Roosevelt and the fact that he was not a Republican greatly enhanced his chances for election as president in 1932. He had a great love for his country, and he had a plan to help the nation recover from the economic depression.

**His personal philosophy.** Franklin Roosevelt's thinking was undoubtedly influenced by his father. James Roosevelt was a Democrat with conservative tendencies and had been a diplomat under President Cleveland. He influenced his son to develop courage and positive decision making. James Roosevelt strongly emphasized the principle of not allowing special interest groups to force one into making decisions. This background laid the foundation for his son's political career.

Another person who heavily influenced Franklin's outlook on life was his distant cousin, Theodore Roosevelt, who was also from New York. Theodore Roosevelt was the twenty-sixth president of the United States. In addition to both men becoming presidents, both were outdoorsmen and continually returned to estates in New York for recreation and relaxation during their careers. Both men had physical handicaps; Franklin's was polio, Theodore's was asthma. Theodore and Franklin had private tutors while growing up and were taught to work hard and to give fair and unprejudiced treatment to all people. Both loved their country and believed in firm action to defend it when necessary. Also, the Roosevelt cousins attended Harvard University and Columbia Law School and served as assistants to the secretary of the navy. Both Roosevelts also used dramatics extremely well in the political arena. The two men ran for the office of vice president, and both began their political careers in the state of New York.

A political difference between the two men was that Theodore was a Republican and Franklin a Democrat. Yet, Franklin Roosevelt greatly admired his older cousin and was not hesitant to adopt some of his progressive ideas in politics. He initiated programs involving risks, he tried new ideas, and changed outmoded traditional programs. He also increased the efficiency of the government to improve the nation's fiscal and social conditions.

## THE PROGRAM OF THE NEW DEAL

Before he was elected president, Franklin D. Roosevelt had promised the people a "New Deal." The New Deal was a set of policies that was produced from the ideas of Theodore Roosevelt and Woodrow Wilson and was mixed with Franklin Roosevelt's own philosophy. The New Deal promised that injustices within the business and financial communities would be controlled, and agriculture and labor groups were promised more welfare relief. Roosevelt's New Deal was not a radical move to socialism as some claimed, but was rather a shift toward a more middle-ground course of action.

**Practical promises.** Franklin Roosevelt's plan was to distribute the nation's abundance broadly to those in need. He determined that if the private sector would not find a way to solve the nation's economic problems, then the government would solve them. In his first inaugural address, Roosevelt began his psychological attack on the depression with his famous phrase, "The only thing we have to fear is fear itself." This phrase was to become a source of encouragement to the nation throughout the Roosevelt administration. In his address, Roosevelt called for strict control of banking and credit, a work project that would employ many jobless citizens, and a Good Neighbor Policy in world affairs.

The people of the United States needed the encouragement Roosevelt's talk gave. Their response to his words was overwhelmingly positive; they were ready to accept the challenge for discipline, duty, and a return to values of high morality. Many people believed that the nation had fallen into sin in the 1920s and was now reaping what it had sown.

In President Roosevelt's New Deal, the emphasis was to build from the bottom up, not from the top down. The key to the program was the hard-working common man. Farmers, small banks and businesses, and average homeowners were among those who would be helped. Tariff reduction would also be sought to encourage international trade. Roosevelt declared publicly that he was going to try bold experiments; if one experiment did not work, he would attempt another.

To carry out the details of his New Deal, Roosevelt carefully selected a cabinet of competent people. Much of the success of his plan depended on the loyalty and hard work of these individuals. They had to believe in the ability of their president, and they must have confidence in his goals. Although this cabinet included individuals of a variety of political persuasions and experiences, it constituted an important part in the success of the New Deal.

**Positive action.** President Roosevelt intended to put his plans for national recovery into immediate action. As soon as his term in office began, Roosevelt initiated his First Hundred Days program. This program stressed passing as much legislation as soon as possible; any legislative action at all was better than the economic standstill the nation was experiencing.

One of the first things Roosevelt did as president was to get Congress to pass the Emergency Banking Act. This act prevented panic withdrawals of funds from banks by the public. The act also called for the banks to close, be evaluated by the government, and reopen only if approved as being fiscally sound.

President Roosevelt gave the first of his famous "fireside chats" on March 12, 1933. He assured the people that their money would be safer "...in a reopened bank than under the mattress." The president's efforts caused people to regain confidence in the nation's banking system and to stop hoarding money. A steady flow of money began to return to most banks. Only five percent of the banks closed permanently. The Emergency Banking Act was not an effort to nationalize banks as some supposed; on the contrary, the government saved the nation's private banks. The act also removed the nation's currency from the gold standard; the people could no longer pay or demand payment in gold.

In attempting to reduce unemployment from a figure of twelve million, Congress established the Civilian Conservation Corps. This organization gave jobs to young men between seventeen and twenty-five years of age. These young men received thirty dollars a month for planting trees, maintaining parks, and doing various building projects. Many of the hundreds of thousands who entered this program also received meals, housing, and clothing.

Congress passed the Federal Emergency Relief Act on May 12. Five hundred million dollars were made available to individual states for relief to the unemployed. Much of this money was given out as work relief, giving people a sense of worth and dignity as they earned their checks.

The Agricultural Adjustment Act was passed in May and gave farm prices "equality of purchasing power." This act gave farmers higher prices for less production, and they were paid not to farm certain amounts of acreage of crops such as wheat, cotton, corn, tobacco, and rice, or to produce more than specified quotas of hogs, milk, and milk products.

This principle of restriction bothered most farmers, but they accepted it as a temporary measure to help the economy and themselves. Because of legal problems, a modification of the same act was passed in 1936 to replace the Agricultural Adjustment Act. The main addition provided that farmers who practiced soil conservation would be paid by the government for doing so. Another bill, commonly referred to as the second Agricultural Adjustment Act, was passed in 1938. In addition to paying farmers not to produce certain acreage, this second Agricultural Adjustment Act provided for surplus crops to be bought and stored by the government for bad years that might come. A similar program was used quite well by Jacob's son, Joseph, to avert starvation during the famine days in Egypt (Genesis 41).

Agriculture was getting the help it needed, but the nation's industry was still in an extremely critical position. On June 16, 1933, Congress passed the National Industrial Recovery Act aimed at business standards used by various industries. The petty, prejudiced, and merciless practices of competition that were common in the years immediately preceding the depression had to be eliminated. Private companies and the federal government were asked to form fair business codes together. Included in these codes were minimum and maximum prices, production controls, credit terms, and other needed codes. However, by May of 1935, the act was declared unconstitutional. Industry refused to control prices, purchasing power did not increase, and the competition standards practiced by many companies were inconsistent. Although the National Industrial Recovery Act had little effect on the recovery of the nation's economy, it did influence such changes as minimum and maximum wages, the abuse of child labor, and **collective bargaining** for workers.

On August 5, 1935, the Social Security Act was signed. The demands for the distribution of wealth and support for the aged caused the New Deal to break with the tradition of letting families provide for their elderly. The Social Security Act provided for old age pensions, old age insurance, unemployment insurance, and a number of other public health programs. Social Security was handled solely by the federal government, although employees and employers paid into it. Many people were financially helped by this act, and the morale of the country was significantly raised.

President Roosevelt had been interested in natural resource conservation for many years. Because of this interest, the Tennessee Valley Authority was approved. Thirty dams were built on the Tennessee River and its tributaries to provide flood control and other benefits. After the dams were built, boats were able to navigate the Tennessee River from Paducah, Kentucky, to Knoxville, Tennessee, a distance of some 630 miles. Soil was

improved in that area because grass and trees were planted, in addition to crops, to prevent soil erosion. The Tennessee Valley Authority lowered charges for electricity and greatly helped the rebuilding of the Tennessee Valley's economy. Other conservation projects were carried out in the northwest and southwest regions of our country.

After his overwhelming victory in 1936, President Roosevelt had to protect his New Deal from the opposition of the United States Supreme Court. The Court had continually rejected measures of the New Deal as unconstitutional, hindering the program greatly. Roosevelt was worried that the nine justices were too conservative and growing too old. He wanted to appoint six additional justices as the nine members passed seventy years of age. However, this plan to have fifteen Supreme Court justices was met with vigorous resistance. Although his idea failed, the Supreme Court decisions tended to be less harsh against the New Deal. Also, as conservative justices died, they were replaced by more liberal thinking men. Roosevelt had lost a battle, but he was beginning to win the war.

In the 1930s many people had only enough money to buy food. They were unable to secure automobiles, a college education, or medical and dental services. In some areas of our nation, people paid bills with produce and personal items.

President Roosevelt's New Deal specifically dealt with the plight of minorities in the United States, especially African-Americans, Mexican-Americans, and Native Americans. The New Deal for minorities was administered by such individuals as Harold Ickes, former president of the Chicago Chapter of the National Association for the Advancement of Colored People and Eleanor Roosevelt, the president's wife. Some of their goals for improved conditions were to cut down the unemployment level of African-Americans, to help the thousands of farm tenants and **sharecroppers** who lost their land, to help minorities receive better wages, and to improve the living conditions of migrant workers.

President Roosevelt's foreign policy was similar to that of Woodrow Wilson's. Roosevelt sought world peace and strove to have a Good Neighbor Policy. He was able to develop a working relationship with Canada in the north and Latin American countries in the south. He did not have as much success with Europe and Asia, however. President Roosevelt personally spoke to representatives of the Nazi and Japanese powers, and he also wrote letters condemning their actions leading to another global war. As his attempts for peace failed, the president increased the nation's preparation for war. Through fireside chats, press conferences and messages to Congress, President Roosevelt endeavored to keep the people informed and to prepare the people for the coming conflict.

By the end of the 1930s, the United States was recovering well from the depression. The progress from the eight years of Roosevelt's New Deal was very evident. Although millions of people were still out of work, the positive action of Roosevelt's program had put millions of others back to work. The president had inspired a discouraged people, and the people had begun to see that conditions were better.

The end of the depression, however, came when World War II ended the nation's economic problems. Formerly unemployed people would either be in military service, have work supporting the war effort, or take positions servicemen had vacated. War is not a desirable solution to a country's economic problems, but it does help remedy the depressed economy of an industrial nation. Such was the case of the United States at the end of the 1930s.

**True/False.**

4.1 _____ Franklin Roosevelt's father was a wealthy railroad man.

4.2 _____ Roosevelt was Secretary of the Navy under President Wilson.

4.3 _____ Franklin Roosevelt served two terms as a state senator.

4.4 _____ President Roosevelt began his New Deal by initiating his First Hundred Days program.

4.5 _____ Roosevelt's informal radio talks were called "fireside chats."

4.6 _____ The Social Security Act, passed in 1933, provided for corporation health programs for employees to be handled by the corporations.

4.7 _____ President Roosevelt's foreign policy was similar to that of Woodrow Wilson's.

4.8 _____ Roosevelt's Good Neighbor Policy did not fare well.

4.9 _____ President Roosevelt was not concerned with most minorities.

4.10 _____ Harold Ickes and Eleanor Roosevelt led the fight to help minorities.

**Choose the best answers.**

4.11     What were six similarities of the two Roosevelts?

      _____ a.  both attended Yale
      _____ b.  both ran for vice president
      _____ c.  both were assistants to the secretary of the navy
      _____ d.  both were state politicians in Ohio
      _____ e.  both went to Columbia University Law School
      _____ f.  both attended Harvard
      _____ g.  both became president
      _____ h.  both were Republicans
      _____ i.  both were private tutors
      _____ j.  both had physical handicaps

**Match the following.**

4.12   _____   Emergency Banking Act         a. work relief for states

4.13   _____   Federal Emergency Relief Act     b. prevented panic withdrawals

4.14   _____   Agriculture Adjustment Act      c. improved business ethics

4.15   _____   National Industrial Recovery Act   d. equality for farm prices

4.16   _____   Tennessee Valley Authority      e. electrical power and soil conservation

**Answer the following question.**

4.17     As a United States citizen in 1932, what preparation of Roosevelt's made him the man you wanted for president?

_____

_____

_____

_____

_____

_____

_____

**Adult Check**   _____

                             **Initial**        **Date**

**Fill in the blanks.**

4.18    President Roosevelt had been governor of the state of _____ .

4.19    Roosevelt was elected president in _____ .

4.20    Roosevelt was determined to become stronger after he contracted _____ .

4.21    Roosevelt's New Deal grew out of the ideas of Presidents _____ and
        _____ .

4.22    President Roosevelt decided that if the private sector could not solve the nation's economic
        problems, then the _____ would.

4.23    The emphasis in Roosevelt's New Deal was to build from the _____ .

4.24    What was Roosevelt's famous phrase that encouraged the country throughout his administration?
        " _____ "


**Match these vocabulary words with their definitions.**

4.25    _____ apropos

4.26    _____ collective bargaining

4.27    _____ sharecropper

a. A tenant farmer who pays a share of his crop as rent for
   his land

b. Negotiation between organized workers and employers
   on wages, hours, conditions, and benefits

c. Suited to the time, place or occasion


**Adult Check**    _____
                   **Initial        Date**


Before you take this last Self Test, you may want to do one or more of these self checks.

1. _____ Read the objectives. Determine if you can do them.

2. _____ Restudy the material related to any objectives that you cannot do.

3. _____ Use the SQ3R study procedure to review the material:
   a. **S**can the sections.
   b. **Q**uestion yourself again (review the questions you wrote initially).
   c. **R**ead to answer your questions.
   d. **R**ecite the answers to yourself.
   e. **R**eview areas you didn't understand.

4. _____ Review all vocabulary, activities and Self Tests, writing a correct answer
   for each wrong answer.

# SELF TEST 4

**Match each of these items with the description that fits them best** (each answer, 2 points).

4.01 _____ New Deal

a. legislation controlling corporation competition practices

4.02 _____ First Hundred Days

b. evaluation of national banks

4.03 _____ Emergency Banking Act

c. Roosevelt's recovery program

4.04 _____ Federal Emergency Relief Act

d. Roosevelt's initial program to pass as much legislation as possible

4.05 _____ Agricultural Adjustment Act

e. financial aid for homeowners

4.06 _____ National Industrial Recovery Act

f. provided jobs in conservation

4.07 _____ Social Security Act

g. direct relief for needy under Hoover

4.08 _____ Tennessee Valley Authority

h. five million dollars in work relief

4.09 _____ Reconstruction Finance Corporation

i. legislation controlling farm prices

4.010 _____ Home Loan Bank System

j. program of flood control and soil conservation

4.011 _____ Civilian Conservation Corps

k. care and support for aged

**Match the significance of the following terms and events** (each answer, 2 points).

4.012 _____ Eighteenth Amendment

a. banned the buying and selling of liquor in the United States

4.013 _____ Treaty of Versailles

b. led to the United States involvement in World War I

4.014 _____ sinking of *Lusitania*

c. led to German surrender in World War I

4.015 _____ assassination of Ferdinand

d. led to Austria declaring war on Serbia, beginning World War I

4.016 _____ surrender of German allies

e. peace signed by Germany after World War I

**True/False** (each answer, 1 point).

4.017 _____ Theodore Roosevelt and Woodrow Wilson influenced Franklin Roosevelt's New Deal ideas.

4.018 _____ Franklin Roosevelt purposed to put his plans for national recovery into action immediately.

4.019 _____ Hoover put too much hope in the private sector pulling the United States out of the Great Depression.

4.020 _____ The Civilian Conservation Corps and the Tennessee Valley Authority provided jobs during the depression.

4.021 _____ Franklin Roosevelt appointed six additional justices of the Supreme Court.

4.022 _____ Although Roosevelt helped the nation's morale, his programs did little to pull the United States out of the Great Depression.

4.023 _____ Coolidge and Hoover failed to take measures to prevent the coming depression.

4.024 _____ Better wages, entertainment, and opportunities for advancement drew many people to the cities.

**Choose the best answers** (each answer, 2 points).

4.025 Mark three ways the attitudes of the United States changed after World War I from what they were before the war.

_____ a. lost interest in progressive causes
_____ b. had more interest in progressive causes
_____ c. they wanted to return to a normal lifestyle
_____ d. they were not concerned with the question of isolationism or internationalism
_____ e. the question of isolationism or internationalism was a major concern

**Answer the following question** (4 points).

4.026 How did Roosevelt's background prepare him for the difficulties of the depression years?

_____

_____

_____

_____

40 / 50

**Score**
**Adult Check** _____
                    **Initial**        **Date**

Before you take the LIFEPAC Test, you may want to do one or more of these self checks.

1. _____ Read the objectives. Determine if you can do them.
2. _____ Restudy the material related to any objectives that you cannot do.
3. _____ Use the SQ3R study procedure to review the material.
4. _____ Review all activities and Self Tests and LIFEPAC Glossary.
5. _____ Restudy areas of weakness indicated by the last Self Test.